ANIMALS ARE WILD!

WEIRD ANIMALS

STEVE PARKER

Gareth Stevens
PUBLISHING

Please visit our website, www.garethstevens.com.
For a free color catalog of all our high-quality books, call toll free 1-800-542-2595 or fax 1-877-542-2596

Cataloging-in-Publication Data

Names: Parker, Steve.
Title: Weird animals / Steve Parker.
Description: New York : Gareth Stevens Publishing, 2016. | Series: Animals are wild! | Includes index.
Identifiers: ISBN 9781482449983 (pbk.) | ISBN 9781482450002 (library bound) | ISBN 9781482449990 (6 pack)
Subjects: LCSH: Animals--Juvenile literature.
Classification: LCC QL49.P37 2016 | DDC 591--dc23

Published in 2017 by
Gareth Stevens Publishing
111 East 14th Street, Suite 349
New York, NY 10003

Copyright © 2017 Miles Kelly Publishing LtdPublishing Director Belinda Gallagher

Creative Director Jo Cowan
Editorial Director Rosie Neave
Senior Editor Claire Philip
Concept Designer Simon Lee
Designers Joe Jones, Rob Hale
Image Manager Liberty Newton
Production Manager Elizabeth Collins
Reprographics Stephan Davis, Thom Allaway
Assets Lorraine King

ACKNOWLEDGMENTS:
The publishers would like to thank the following sources for the use of their photographs:
Key: (m) = main (i) = inset
Front cover: (main) Dennis Avon/ardea.com, (Wild Nature animal globe) ranker/Shutterstock.com
Back cover: (top) Fedor Selivanov/Shutterstock.com, (bottom) John A. Anderson/Shutterstock.com
Page 1 Radka Palenikova/Shutterstock.com
Pages 4–5 (clockwise from bottom left) Juniors Bildarchiv/Photolibrary.com, Barry Mansell/Photolibrary.com,
Jen & Des Bartlett/Photolibrary.com, Michael Moxter/Photolibrary.com, Corbis/Photolibrary.com
Page 1 Teguh Tirtaputra/Shutterstock.com
Jackson's chameleon (m) Corbis/Photolibrary.com, (i) Solvin Zankl/naturepl.com
Porcupine fish (m) J. W. Alker/Imagebroker/FLPA, (i) Norbert Probst/Imagebroker/FLPA
Aardvark (m) Frans Lanting/FLPA, (i) Owen Newman/naturepl.com
Peacock mantis shrimp (m) Chris Newbert/FLPA, (i) Solvin Zankl/naturepl.com
Short-beaked echidna (m) Cyril Ruoso/FLPA, (i) Steven David Miller/naturepl.com
Goldenrod crab spider (m) Nick Garbutt/naturepl.com
Giraffe weevil (m) Michael Krabs/Imagebroker/FLPA
Knobbed hornbill (m) Tui De Roy/FLPA, (i) Tim Laman/naturepl.com
Frilled lizard (m) Michael & Patricia Fogden/FLPA, (i) ANT Photo Library/NHPA
Vampire bat (m) Michael & Patricia Fogden/FLPA, (i) Jim Clare/naturepl.com
Platypus (m) Dave Watts/naturepl.com (i) Dave Watts/naturepl.com
Three-banded armadillo (m) Mark Payne-Gill/naturepl.com (i) Mark Payne-Gill/naturepl.com
Pot-belly seahorse (m) George Grall/Getty Images
Tyron's sea slug (m) Colin Marshall/FLPA
Naked mole rat (m) Raymond Mendez/Photolibrary.com, (i) Neil Bromhall/naturepl.com
Ecuador tree frog (m) Pete Oxford/FLPA (i) Pete Oxford/FLPA
Tuatara (m) Pete Oxford/naturepl.com, (i) Mark Moffett/FLPA
Hoatzin (m) Pete Oxford/naturepl.com, (i) Flip De Nooyer/FLPA
Stalk-eyed fly (m) Mark Moffett/FLPA, (i) Phil Savoie/naturepl.com
Proboscis monkey (m) Nick Garbutt/naturepl.com
Every effort has been made to acknowledge the source and copyright holder of each picture.
Miles Kelly Publishing apologizes for any unintentional errors or omissions.

Printed in the United States of America

CPSIA compliance information: Batch CS16GS:
For further information contact Gareth Stevens, New York, New York at 1-800-542-2595.

CONTENTS

BIZARRE BITS? NORMAL FOR ME!

↓ Bats navigate by listening to the echoes of their own squeaks and clicks. Bigger ears mean better hearing and a safer flight path.

What huge ears! Look at those bizarre horns! Odd feet, strange noses, peculiar tails... some animals are very weird indeed, and quite unlike other creatures.

Animals have unusual features for good reasons. In the wild, anything that gives an advantage over rivals may be key to survival. So really big ears may catch the faintest sounds to locate food, while spines or armor protect against predators.

Other features may be used to attract and impress potential mates. When creatures get together at breeding time, what seems really weird to us looks totally appealing to their own kind.

1

→ The proboscis monkey's big floppy snout is partly for smell. Its size also tells other monkeys: "I'm grown up and ready to breed."

FUNNY FACES

Most animals have their main sensing parts for sight, hearing, smell and taste on the head. So an extra-big nose for smell, or an extra-long tongue to taste and gather food is a good tactic, even if it does make the face look misshapen.

GIANT NOSE

→ The pangolin doesn't have to run from enemies because its scales provide such good protection.

SCALY SAFE

3 SELF-DEFENSE

Hunting animals usually have big teeth, claws or other weapons that they can use for attack or defense. Plant eaters need other kinds of protection, such as being able to look bigger, or fiercer, or spikier – or all of these.

4 MATING TIME

Some of the weirdest body features are there to attract partners and frighten off rivals. Many animals put on crazy displays to show off their assets, in the hope of getting the attention of a potential partner.

PICK ME!

↖ The sea slug's warning colors are designed to get them noticed. They tell predators: "Don't eat me, I taste horrible."

YUCKY TASTE

2 ODD BODIES

Different body shapes suit different lifestyles. In particular, being the same color and pattern as your surroundings, known as camouflage, is great for hiding from predators and for sneaking up on prey.

← The male great frigatebird puffs up his throat skin like a red balloon to attract nearby female birds.

Very slowly, the chameleon creeps along the branch, relying on its incredibly tiny movements and amazing camouflage to remain unnoticed by its insect prey. This strangest of lizards rocks its body slightly to gauge distance with its swiveling eyes. Then, faster than the human eye can follow, it flicks out its immensely long, slimy tongue. The fly is caught on the sticky, suction-cup tip, and the chameleon leisurely chews its latest meal.

HORNED MONSTER

'STAR FACT

Most chameleons lay eggs, but Jackson's chameleon gives birth to live young. Within hours of being born the babies are practicing their hunting skills on tiny prey such as mosquitoes.

DOWN IN ONE...

This Namaqua desert chameleon has just caught a beetle. Its sticky tongue flicks into its mouth and the hard-cased, spiky victim will be crushed, slurped and swallowed in seconds.

SPECIAL FEATURES

HORNS: The male's horns are mostly for show, to frighten enemies and impress females when breeding, but they can be jabbed at attackers.

CAMOUFLAGE: Chameleons can change color. The colors indicate moods such as anger or fright, and are sometimes for camouflage, too.

Jackson's chameleon

Scientific name: *Chamaeleo jacksonii*
Type: Reptile
Lifespan: 3-5 years
Length: 11.8 in (30 cm)
Weight: Up to 1.1 lb (500 g)
Range: East Africa
Status: Not assessed

WOW...

Each eye turret swivels through almost a full half circle, independent of the other eye, so the chameleon can look to the front and rear at the same time!

TONGUE: A typical chameleon has a tongue about two-thirds as long as its body. It can flick out, catch prey on its sticky tip and return in one-fifth of a second.

FEET: The weird feet each have five toes that are fused (joined) into two groups of two and three, like a pincer, to give excellent branch-gripping power.

This strange fish gulps in water to make its body swell up, becoming as round and hard as a football. Once it has done so, predators will have problems even getting a bite of the porcupinefish, never mind trying to swallow it. The sharp, thornlike growths in its skin usually lie flat against its body. But as the fish swells, the spines tilt and start to poke outwards, putting off the predator even more.

SPIKY SWIMMER

A water-swallowing fish takes only seconds to enlarge into a ball. But deflating back to its normal shape can take several minutes.

BACK TO NORMAL...

SPECIAL FEATURES

SWIMMING: Porcupinefish and their relatives are very agile swimmers, moving sideways and even backwards as they forage for food.

BEAK: A porcupinefish's teeth are solidly fused into a hard, strong beak that can crush prey such as sea snails, clams and mussels.

Porcupinefish

Scientific name: *Cyclichthys*
(several species)
Type: Fish
Lifespan: Unknown in the wild
Length: 7.9 in (20 cm)
Weight: 3.5–5.3 oz (100–150 g)
Range: Southeast Atlantic,
Indian and West Pacific Oceans
Status: Not assessed

'STAR FACT

Many porcupinefish hide in cracks in the reef, and in the chambers inside sponges (large marine animals without backbones) during the day, emerging at night to feed.

OUCH...

The fish's strong protective spines have very sharp tips. They are made from a material similar to that of the rods or rays that hold out and wave the fins.

EYES: Its large eyes are adapted for seeing in the dark, as this porcupinefish is nocturnal. It hunts over mud and sand and also among reef rocks and corals.

SKIN: The spines are fixed into strong, tough skin that is also stretchy enough to allow the fish to expand as it "puffs up" with water.

As the heat and light fade on the dry African grasslands, a strange creature shuffles and snorts inside its 40-foot (12 m) burrow. The aardvark's long nose resembles that of an anteater, and its excellent senses of hearing and smell are tuned to the tiny scrabbling sounds and scent of the insects that make up nearly all of its diet – ants and termites. Hungry after a day's sleep, on a good night the aardvark's long, snakelike tongue will lick up more than 50,000 of its tiny prey.

DIGGER CHAMP

WAKE UP...

The aardvark shelters in its burrow by day, and emerges at dusk to begin its night of foraging.

SPECIAL FEATURES

FUR AND SKIN: A furry coat of coarse hairs, plus tough leathery skin, provide good protection while burrowing and against predators.

FEET AND CLAWS: The feet have big claws that resemble a combination of nail and hoof, for breaking into the hardest of termite mounds.

Aardvark

Scientific name: *Orycteropus afer*
Type: Mammal
Lifespan: 10-15 years
Length: 6.7 ft (2 m)
Weight: 110-130 lb (50-60 kg)
Range: Most of Africa south of the Sahara
Status: Least concern

SCRAM...

One of the fastest animal burrowers, an aardvark confronted by an enemy out in the open can dig its way out of danger, disappearing into the soil in a few seconds.

TEETH: Its small jaws have only molar (cheek) teeth. These have an unusual layered structure, are quite soft and regrow continuously as they wear down.

NOSE: The very long snout houses exceptionally sensitive smell detectors, while the nostrils can close in a split second to prevent clogging with soil.

With the impact of a bullet and lightning speed, the brightly colored mantis shrimp jabs out its club-like second legs to bash its hard-cased prey to bits. Sea snails, crabs, clams and similar shellfish, other types of shrimps and prawns – nothing can withstand one of nature's fastest, most forceful attacks. No wonder human divers who are unlucky enough to experience their bludgeoning blows refer to these shrimps as "thumbsplitters."

SHELL STRIKER

'STAR FACT

Mantis shrimps are surprisingly clever creatures. They can remember the locations of hidden food, rather than just relying on sight and smell, and will even move obstacles to get at it.

SMASH AND GRAB....

After smashing the hermit crab's shell, the mantis shrimp simply pulls the poor creature from its hiding place, hits it repeatedly to subdue it, then starts to feast on its soft body.

SPECIAL FEATURES

LEGS: Three pairs of walking legs allow the shrimp to scuttle along quickly. The seven pairs behind them have paddle-like flaps for swimming.

HAMMERS: The second pair of limbs are like spring-loaded hammers that flick out with dizzying speed at both prey and predators.

Peacock mantis shrimp

Scientific name: *Odontodactylus scyllarus*
Type: Crustacean
Lifespan: Possibly 5-10 years
Length: Up to 9.8 in (25 cm)
Weight: 1.1 lb (500 g)
Range: Indian and West Pacific Oceans
Status: Not enough information

READY...

With its deadly hammer-legs at the ready, folded in a manner similar to the praying mantis insect, the mantis shrimp eyes its next target – you!

EYES: Its mobile, stalked eyes have detailed color vision and can judge distance accurately, so the shrimp relies mainly on sight when hunting.

ANTENNAE: Two pairs of long antennae detect objects by touch, sense water currents, and scent floating substances in a form of underwater smelling.

It is covered in spines and it eats ants, so the echidna is sometimes known as "spiny anteater," and it is a very unusual kind of mammal. It lays eggs, like a bird. Its young develop in the female's pouch, like a kangaroo. In cold conditions it lowers its body temperature to just a few degrees above freezing, like a hibernating dormouse. And it can dig itself out of sight into the ground in seconds, like a mole.

PRICKLE-TOP

Just like a hedgehog, the echidna can roll into a spiky ball that few predators can undo.

GO AWAY . . .

SPECIAL FEATURES

FRONT CLAWS: Big foreclaws enable the echidna to dig burrows for shelter and to rip into hard-walled termite mounds and ant nests.

BACK CLAWS: The echidna uses its long, curved rear claws to groom or comb its fur and prickles, removing dirt and any pests, such as fleas.

Short-beaked echidna

Scientific name: *Tachyglossus aculeatus*
Type: Mammal
Lifespan: 40-45 years
Length: 16-18 in (40-45 cm)
Weight: 6.6-8.8 lb (3-4 kg)
Range: Australia, New Guinea
Status: Least concern

YIKES...

'STAR FACT

The female echidna lays a single grape-sized egg straight into a pocket-like pouch on her underside. It hatches after ten days into a tiny, helpless baby.

The 500-plus prickles are made of very thick, long, strong, sharp hairs. Normal furry hairs between them keep the echidna warm.

SNOUT: Very long and narrow, the snout is excellent for smelling food. But the mouth is as small as this "O," unable to bite, so the echidna relies on its...

TONGUE: The 8-inch (20 cm) tongue flicks in and out up to 100 times each minute. Its sticky coating picks up food such as ants and termites.

The fly scans the flower for danger. All seems clear so it lands, ready to sip sweet nectar. Then... *jump, kick, grab, stab!* As if from nowhere the camouflaged crab spider topples the fly with a well-aimed kick. Gripping the victim with its legs, the spider stabs its fangs into the fly's body and injects poison and digestive juices. These paralyze the victim and gradually turn its insides into soupy mush for the spider to suck up.

HIDDEN KILLER

Goldenrod crab spider

Scientific name: *Misumena vatia*
Type: Arachnid
Lifespan: Unknown, possibly 5 years
Length: Male 0.16 in (4 mm), female 0.4 in (11 mm)
Range: Northern temperate lands
Status: Not enough information

STAR FACT

The goldenrod crab spider changes its body color to match the color of its chosen flower. Over the course of a few days, it could go from white, to yellow, to pale green.

BEWARE...

Much larger than the male, the female crab spider crouches among the petals of her flower, matching their colors in every detail.

SPECIAL FEATURES

LEGS: Like all members of its group, crab spiders have eight legs, but these are unusual because they bend to give a sideways motion, like a real crab.

FANGS: The crab spider's fangs are long and slim, designed for piercing the exoskeletons (hard outer body casings) of a wide range of insects.

LONG NECK

Weevils are types of beetles and most have long snouts, but the giraffe weevil goes one better. The males of this species have enormously elongated necks. In the breeding season rival males face each other to gain females and win territories (areas in which they can live and breed). Females prefer longer-necked partners, so the parading males show off to impress, and be chosen.

ME, ME...

The male lifts and sticks out his amazing neck, and nods it up and down at the middle joint, to display his size and strength to any watching females.

Giraffe weevil

Scientific name:
Trachelophorus giraffa
Type: Insect
Lifespan: Unknown, probably 1–2 years
Length: Up to 1.2 in (3 cm)
Range: Madagascar
Status: Not enough information

STAR FACT

Giraffe weevils are usually found on one particular species of tree, where they feed and breed. For this reason, this type of tree is known as the giraffe weevil tree.

SPECIAL FEATURES

NECK: The female also has a fairly long neck. This helps when building her nest of rolled-up leaves, in which she lays her single egg.

WINGS: The weevil's front pair of wings are protective covers. The second pair of flimsy flying wings are folded beneath them.

This big, strong bird is probably named because its huge beak, or bill, looks similar to the horn of a cow. The hornbill's amazing bill is covered in keratin (a tough, lightweight material) and has many uses, from feeding and preening to pecking enemies, and the female uses it to mix chewed food and droppings into a paste. She uses this paste for a strange purpose – to wall off the entrance to her nest hole, trapping herself inside. Only a narrow slit is left, through which the male passes food and she ejects droppings.

MEGA BEAK

The male hornbill supplies all of the female's food while she is trapped inside the nest hole.

TRAPPED...

SPECIAL FEATURES

FLIGHT: Despite their large size, hornbills fly strongly on their long, powerful wings, with noisy, whooshing wingbeats.

NECK: The two uppermost neck bones are joined or fused, and the neck has very strong muscles, so the bird can move its huge bill very accurately.

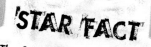

Knobbed hornbill

Scientific name: *Aceros cassidix*
Type: Bird
Lifespan: 25-30 years
Length: 31.5-35.4 in (80-90 cm)
Weight: 4.4 lb (2 kg)
Range: Southeast Asia, mainly Sulawesi
Status: Least concern

YUMMY...

With expert precision the hornbill plucks small berries, seeds, buds and similar items, ready to toss them up in the air and swallow them.

SIGHT: Its two eyes face partly forwards and can see along the tapering bill to its tip, which allows the hornbill to peck and pick up food with great precision.

BILL: The hugely useful beak, and the red casque (ridge) on top, are not quite as heavy as they look, being partly honeycomb-like with air spaces inside.

One of nature's weirdest sights is a frightened frilled lizard trying to scare off an enemy. The lizard gapes its mouth wide and erects the wide frill of skin around its neck to make itself look bigger and more menacing. It also stands up stiff-legged and swishes its tail, hissing loudly. This defensive display makes most predators think twice. As they do so, the lizard suddenly turns tail, races away and leaps to safety in the branches of a nearby tree.

FRILLED DEFENDER

Its long, muscular back legs carry the frilled lizard along almost as fast as you could run, but only for a short distance.

RACE...

CAMOUFLAGE: Dull browns and greens give the frilled lizard excellent camouflage in its woodland habitat.

MOUTH: The wide mouth has small but strong teeth to grab and chew beetles, cicadas, ants and similar, small-but-tough prey.

Frilled lizard

Scientific name: *Chlamydosaurus kingii*
Type: Reptile
Lifespan: 10-15 years
Length: 35.4 in (90 cm)
Weight: 1.1 lb (500 g)
Range: North Australia, New Guinea
Status: Least concern

STAR FACT

Frilled lizards hunt in trees for bugs such as caterpillars and spiders. They also prowl on the ground for insects, worms, and the occasional mouse, baby bird or smaller lizard.

HISS...

The brightly colored frill, like a scaly umbrella, contrasts with the lizard's dull body color. The frill measures up to 7.9 inches (20 cm) across.

FRILL: The wide frill of leathery skin is held out by rods of gristle (cartilage). Usually it lies flat along the lizard's neck and shoulders.

FEET AND CLAWS: Very long toes and sharp, curved claws give the lizard great non-slip grip even on the smoothest, slipperiest bark.

Dusk falls and farm animals settle down to sleep. Then a shadow flits silently into the cowshed and lands on the ground – a vampire bat. With strange, scuttling movements it hops and scurries towards its victim. After a few seconds in which it snips away hairs to reach the cow's bare skin, the bat uses its sharp teeth to slice a neat, shallow, rounded wound, which starts to bleed. Special chemicals in its saliva keep the blood flowing, and the bat sets to work to suck and lap up its nighttime snack.

SLICING SUCKER

During a 20-30 minute feed, a vampire bat may take in half of its own body weight in blood.

DELICIOUS...

SPECIAL FEATURES

ECHOLOCATION: The vampire bat navigates in darkness by listening to the echoes of its own clicks and squeaks bouncing off nearby objects.

SIDE TEETH: The canine and molar teeth at the side and back of the mouth work like scissors to cut hair or fur that might interfere with feeding.

SMILE...

Showing off its upper incisor (front) teeth, which are sharper than a razor, a vampire bat gets ready for action.

Vampire bat

Scientific name: *Desmodus rotundus*
Type: Mammal
Lifespan: 8–11 years
Length: 3.5 in (9 cm)
Weight: 0.1–0.2 lb (50–80 g)
Range: Central and South America
Status: Least concern

FRONT TEETH: Like triangular blades, the upper incisor teeth are always sharp, ready to scoop away a small patch of skin and flesh.

SUCKING: This bat can lap up blood with its tongue or suck blood up using the underside of its tongue pressed down onto its lower lip.

The platypus is famed for its strange features. It has a bill and webbed feet like a duck and lays eggs like a bird, but its furry body and wide, flat tail are more like those of a beaver. Perhaps even stranger is this Australian animal's "sixth sense." Its bill detects tiny pulses of electricity in the water given off by the moving muscles of its prey. So the platypus can find food by touch and electro-sense alone, even in the muddiest, darkest creeks and pools in the middle of the night!

DUCK-FACED DIVER

STAR FACT

Most platypus dives last 20-30 seconds, with occasional rests of a few minutes. Its main prey include worms, pond snails, shrimps, yabbies (crayfish), fish and frogs.

PHEW...

Eating one-fifth of your body weight every 24 hours is tiring. Platypuses swim and dive for food for up to 12 hours a day, usually from dusk until dawn.

SPECIAL FEATURES

TAIL: The wide, round-edged tail helps the rear feet in steering and braking. It also stores food reserves for times when prey is scarce.

FEET: Long, wide-splayed toes with webbed skin between them are ideal for paddling and swimming at the surface and underwater.

Platypus

Scientific name: *Ornithorhynchus anatinus*
Type: Mammal
Lifespan: 10-15 years
Length: Male about 20 in (50 cm), female about 18 in (45 cm)
Weight: Male 4.4 lb (2 kg), female 3.3 lb (1.5 kg)
Range: Eastern Australia
Status: Least concern

The platypus digs one of the longest nesting burrows, more than 65 feet (20 m) into the bank. Here the female lays her two eggs, which hatch into hairless, blind babies that suckle her milk.

HOME AND DRY...

FUR: Its very dense fur traps tiny air bubbles that help the platypus to float upwards, as well as keeping its skin warm and dry.

BILL: The bill is slightly flexible, like thick rubber, and is amazingly sensitive to touch. The mouth is on the underside of the bill.

The armadillo looks like no other living creature. Although it resembles a scaly, plant-eating reptile from the age of dinosaurs, it's actually a warm-blooded mammal. It has fur poking out around the sides of its bony armor, and is a meat eater of sorts, although its main foods are tiny termites, ants, worms and similar creepy-crawlies. It may also snack occasionally on ripe fruits, shoots and buds, or even scavenge the remains of dead animals.

ARMOR-DILLO

MOVE IT...

Armadillos trot along on the clawed tips of their front feet and the flat soles of their back feet.

'STAR FACT

There are 20 different species (kinds) of armadillo, all in the Americas, but only a few, including the three-banded, can roll into a tight ball.

SPECIAL FEATURES

ARMOR: Bony plates called scutes grow within the thickness of the armadillo's skin, covered by outer scales made from horny keratin.

ROLLING UP: The three-banded armadillo's armor is flexible enough for it to curl into a ball, tucking in the head against the tail.

Three-banded armadillo

Scientific name: *Tolypeutes tricinctus*
(Brazilian species)
Type: Mammal
Lifespan: 15 years
Length: 18-20 in (45-50 cm)
Weight: 3.3-4.4 lb (1.5-2 kg)
Range: Northern South America
Status: Vulnerable

HIDE...

After curling up in self-defense, the armadillo waits for several minutes and then opens up slightly to peek out and check that all is clear.

CLAWS: The front feet have massive claws to dig up food, excavate burrows for resting and hiding, and to scratch or slash enemies.

SMELL: Eyesight is poor but the sense of smell is acute, and an armadillo at the surface can scent food down to 8 inches (20 cm) below in the soil.

In the strange world of the sea horse, it's the male who has the babies. The female lays her eggs into a pocket-like pouch on his belly, where they develop over a few weeks. Then the father "gives birth," and 200 or more tiny sea horses emerge. This extraordinary animal has other oddities, too. It is one of the slowest of all fish, using only its back fin to get around, and every morning, a male and female "dance" together to strengthen their partnership.

FISHY HORSE

LOOK...

Each of its bulging eyes can move independently of the other, so the sea horse can look to the front and rear at the same time.

Potbelly sea horse

Scientific name: Hippocampus abdominalis
Type: Fish
Lifespan: 7–10 years
Length: 14 in (35 cm)
Range: Coasts of Australia and New Zealand
Status: Not enough information

STAR FACT

The potbelly sea horse is a bit of a giant, at more than 11.8 inches (30 cm) long. Some species are smaller than this term: "sea horse."

SPECIAL FEATURES

TAIL: A curly prehensile (gripping) tail allows the sea horse to hold onto weeds and rocks so that it can rest and stay safe even in strong currents.

MOUTH: Its mouth is small and tube-like, but the sea horse is still a busy feeder and can swallow more than 5,000 tiny morsels daily.

SLOW AND SLIMY

Sea slugs are among the brightest creatures in the ocean. Also called nudibranchs, they shine as if lit from within as they slime their way across rocks and corals. They are not too worried about predators because their glowing hues are warning colors, showing that their rubbery flesh tastes horrible and may even be poisonous. They spend their days sliding around reefs, feeding at leisure on sponges, and mating occasionally – it's a lazy life.

GLIDE...

A sea slug gets around in the same way as its cousins on land. Waves of rippling muscle contraction pass along its broad base (foot) from tail to head, inching it forwards.

Tryon's sea slug

Scientific name: *Risbecia tryoni*
Type: Mollusc
Lifespan: Unknown, possibly 1-2 years
Length: 2.4 in (6 cm)
Range: West Pacific Ocean
Status: Not enough information

STAR FACT

Sometimes groups of Tryon's sea slugs travel and feed in single file, one after the other. This is known as "tailgating."

SPECIAL FEATURES

TENTACLES: Head tentacles have detectors that sense touch, water movements and currents, and chemical sensors for "smelling" underwater.

TONGUE: Under the head is a tongue, called a radula, that has rows of hundreds of tiny teeth for rubbing at and scraping up food.

Naked mole rats are not moles or rats, but cousins of guinea pigs and porcupines. They spend almost their entire lives in darkness underground, so their eyes barely function. And they have an odd, insect-like way of breeding. Only the queen mole rat gives birth, and she only mates with two or three males. The rest of the 80-strong colony (group) are soldiers that fight enemies, and workers that dig tunnels to gather roots and similar underground plant food.

LIFE IN THE DARK

MUNCH...

Workers gnaw, nibble and bite at the hard, dry earth to make a network of tunnels that might extend more than 2.5 miles (4 km) in total length.

SPECIAL FEATURES

TEETH: The very long, sharp incisor (front) teeth grow continuously as they wear down and self-sharpen as they are used to dig and eat.

LIPS: Lips can close and seal around the teeth even when the mouth is open, so the mole rat does not swallow soil as it tunnels.

Naked mole rat

Scientific name: *Heterocephalus glaber*
Type: Mammal
Lifespan: 25 years, even 28
Length: Worker 3.5 in (9 cm), queen 4.7 in (12 cm)
Weight: Worker 1.1 oz (30 g), queen 2.1 oz (60 g)
Range: East Africa
Status: Least concern

STAR FACT

Newborn mole rats feed on their mother's milk. As the babies develop they move on to eating the droppings of other colony members until they are old enough for proper food.

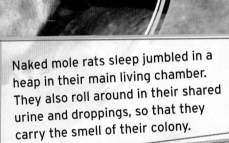

ZZZZZ...

Naked mole rats sleep jumbled in a heap in their main living chamber. They also roll around in their shared urine and droppings, so that they carry the smell of their colony.

LEGS: Short limbs are needed in the cramped burrow, but the legs are very flexible and the mole rat can shuffle backwards as fast as it goes forwards.

SKIN: The mole rat's skin is not quite "naked," in that it has some small hairs, but it is very tough and loose for scraping through tunnels.

Constant moisture makes rain forests the ideal places for frogs of all kinds – especially tree frogs. Among the leaves, the Ecuador tree frog steadies itself on its sucker toes. The special "fly detector" sensors in its huge, bulging eyes are able to spot the tiniest gnat as it buzzes past. In a flash, the frog's head seems to split in half as it opens its enormous mouth and flicks out its long tongue. The tasty morsel is grabbed by the tongue's sticky, curling tip, pulled into the wide-open jaws, and swallowed.

GOGGLE EYES

Male tree frogs make all kinds of croaks, whirrs, chirrups and burps to attract breeding partners.

RIBBIT...

'STAR FACT

The Ecuador tree frog is found in one of the smallest areas of any frog species, in only a few parts of northwest Ecuador and southwest Colombia.

SPECIAL FEATURES

LIMBS: Despite its thinner-than-matchstick legs, this tree frog is surprisingly strong and can pull itself up using just one limb.

TOES: Large, sucker-like pads on the toe tips help to grip even the shiniest, slimiest, slipperiest rain forest leaves and twigs.

Ecuador tree frog

Scientific name: *Hypsiboas (Hyla) picturatus*
(Ecuador, Imbabura or Chachi tree frog)
Type: Amphibian
Lifespan: Unknown, possibly 4-6 years
Length: 0.8-1.2 in (2-3 cm)
Range: Northwest South America
Status: Least concern

WOAH...

The frog's mouth is the widest part of its head, ready to gulp in a meal that can be almost as big as the frog's own body.

EYES: The frog's massive bulging eyes see even the tiniest movements and can also make out certain colors, even in the gloom cast by the forest canopy.

LEAPING: Its rear legs and feet are almost twice as long as the head and body, and have strong muscles for great leaps – usually to escape danger.

It may look like a regular lizard, but the tuatara is actually one of the weirdest of all creatures. Its close cousins were pig-sized, beak-mouthed reptiles called rhynchosaurs that lived alongside early dinosaurs more than 200 million years ago. The tuatara stays cool and lives life slowly. It takes more than 30 years to fully mature, it can hibernate for a year, its eggs may take 16 months to hatch, and some individuals might reach an amazing 150 years of age.

SLOWLY DOES IT

Tuatara

Scientific name: *Sphenodon* (two species)
Type: Reptile
Lifespan: Can exceed 100 years
Length: Male 24 in (60 cm), female 18 in (45 cm)
Weight: Male 2.2 lb (1 kg), female 1.1 lb (0.5 kg)
Range: New Zealand
Status: Vulnerable

COOL...

Most reptiles love to bask in temperatures of greater than 77°F (25°C-plus), but tuataras thrive best at 59-68°F (15-20°C). They are still active at 41°F (5°C), when most reptiles are too chilled to move.

SPECIAL FEATURES

SCALES: The tuatara's scaly plates have an odd structure, similar to a crocodile's plates. They are very tough, providing effective protection.

CREST: The crest of enlarged scales that runs from the head along the back is larger in males and can be held erect when displaying to females.

When it comes to meal times, tuataras are far from slow. They gulp down all kinds of smaller prey, from beetles and spiders to bird eggs and chicks, and even young tuataras!

GRAB AND GULP...

THIRD EYE: Between the two main eyes the tuatara has the remains of a pineal or parietal "third eye." It detects light and dark but cannot form clear images.

TEETH: There are two rows of small teeth in the upper jaw and only one in the lower jaw, ideal for grabbing and chewing struggling victims.

The hoatzin has an abundance of bizarre features. Its body is plump and heavy but its head is tiny. It is a slow, clumsy flier, preferring to clamber among branches to find food. Its diet is mostly leaves, which are difficult to digest, so it has to consume huge amounts – up to one-quarter of its total weight is pecked-off leaves crammed into its guts. Oddest of all, the hoatzin chick has two claws on the front of each wing – a feature seen in prehistoric birds such as *Archaeopteryx* from the dinosaur age but in no other bird alive today.

DINO-BIRD

MY TURN...

Hoatzin parent birds share the burden of raising their young. They take turns to incubate (keep warm) their two or three eggs and then feed the chicks.

HOLD ON...

The young hoatzin uses its wing claws, beak and feet to clamber about in the branches – and to climb back into its nest if it falls out.

SPECIAL FEATURES

FEATHERS: Life in the Amazon rain forest is very damp, but as the hoatzin preens it spreads lots of water-repelling oils onto its feathers.

CALLS: Hoatzins make many kinds of noises from hisses to grunts and loud screams. This helps members of a group to keep together.

'STAR FACT

The way in which the hoatzin digests its green plant food inside its huge gut makes plenty of horrible-smelling gas, earning it the nickname of "stinkbird."

Hoatzin

Scientific name: Opisthocomus hoazin
Type: Bird
Lifespan: 20–25 years
Length: 23.6–27.6 in (60–70 cm)
Weight: 1.8 lb (800 g)
Range: North-Central South America
Status: Least concern

ESCAPE: If a predator approaches, a hoatzin chick will fall out of its nest into the water below. Once danger passes, the chick swims to the bank and climbs back up.

DIGESTION: The enormous bag-like crop – the first part of the gut after the gullet – holds leaves for hours as they ferment (rot) and release their goodness.

Few insects are as strange to look at as the stalk-eyed fly. A close cousin of houseflies and mosquitoes, its body, wings and legs are fairly typical. But the head, especially in the males of the species, has enormously long rod-like stalks, one on each side, each with an eye and antenna (feeler) at the end. The stalks are so long that the distance between a fly's eyes may exceed its body length. Females are impressed by males with long stalks and choose them for breeding.

EYE-TO-FLY

STAR FACT

Long eye stalks are fragile, but as long as females keep choosing males with very wide eye spans, their offspring will continue to inherit the same extreme feature.

HEY, YOU...

Male stalk-eyed flies have eyeball-to-eyeball staring competitions. The one with the widest eye span wins and gets to breed.

SPECIAL FEATURES

LEGS: As well as eyeing up their rival's eye stalks, competing males spread out their front legs and may start to wrestle and kick each other.

EYE STALKS: In some kinds of stalk-eyed flies the male can force air from his mouth along tubes inside the stalks to make them even longer.

Stalk-eyed fly

Scientific name: *Teleopsis, Diopsis, Cyrtodiopsis* and others
Type: Insects
Lifespan: Mostly a few months
Length: 0.08–0.4 in (2–10 mm)
Eye span: 0.08–0.4 in (2–10 mm)
Range: Mostly Africa, South and Southeast Asia
Status: Not assessed

Choosing a mate because of a certain body feature is common in the animal kingdom. Other examples include the male deer's large antlers and the male peacock's spectacular tail.

PICK ME...

EYES: The eyes themselves are fairly normal (for a fly), with hundreds of tiny mosaic-like units that are very sensitive to movement.

MATING: Once a male fly has beaten his rivals, he may mate with up to 20 waiting females in just 20 minutes.

GLOSSARY

burrow a hole made by an animal in which it lives or hides

colony a group of animals living and working together

echolocation a way of locating objects by producing sounds that bounce off objects

exoskeleton the hard outer covering of an animal's body

habitat the natural place where an animal or plant lives

hibernate to be in a sleeplike state for an extended period of time, usually during winter

nocturnal active at night

preen to groom, or clean, feathers

prey an animal that is hunted by other animals for food

species a group of plants or animals that are all of the same kind

FOR MORE INFORMATION

BOOKS

Karr, K. B. *Weird & Wacky Creatures: Strange, Weird Animals That Share Our World!* Grand Rapids, MI: DSG Publishing, 2015.

Sully, Katherine. *Wacky, Wild, and Weird Nature.* New York, NY: Parragon Books, 2013.

WEBSITES

Top 10 Most Unusual Animals on Earth
http://www.funonthenet.in/articles/unusual-animals.html
See photos and learn about some of the strangest animals in the world.

25 Most Bizarre & Fascinating Animal Facts
http://www.globalanimal.org/2015/05/21/25-most-bizarre-fascinating-animal-facts/
Learn 25 amazing facts about weird animals.

INDEX